NIST 800-171:
System Security Plan (SSP)
Template & Workbook
A Supplement to "NIST 800-171: Beyond DOD"

Mark A. Russo, CISSP-ISSAP

The National Institute of Standards and Technology (NIST) special publication series for federal cybersecurity only tells you "what to do." This series of supplements are designed to help you understand "how to" successfully implement the new NIST 800-171 federal government contracting requirements.

FORWARD

This is an ongoing series of supplements we are issuing regarding the changes in federal cybersecurity contracting requirements. It is designed to align with our groundbreaking cybersecurity book: *"NIST 800-171: Beyond DOD"*. Our desire is to provide complete how-to guidance and instruction to effectively and quickly address your businesses' need to secure your Information Technology (IT) environments to effectively compete in the federal contract space. This is designed to be a workbook and template, but much like *"Beyond DOD",* is designed to have best practice information that you can implement immediately. If you want a free soft copy version of the template versions, please reach out to us. We plan to have additional supplements to include the Plan of Action and Milestones (POAM)

 workbook and template. Please keep checking back at Amazon® or reach out to Syber Risk LLC at syber.risk.llc@gmail.com when the next supplements will be released.

We have also prepared a free 36-minute video describing the SSP effort at Udemy.com. The full video can be found under "System Security Plan (SSP) for NIST 800-171 Compliance," https://www.udemy.com/system-security-plan-ssp-for-nist-800-171-compliance/ .

Best to you,

Syber Risk LLC Team

LEGAL STUFF

NIST 800-171: System Security Plan (SSP) Template & Workbook

How does the System Security Plan or SSP meet NIST 800-171 compliance requirements?

There are **110** explicit security controls from NIST 800-171, revision 1, extracted from NIST's core cybersecurity document, NIST 800-53, *Security and Privacy Controls for Federal Information Systems and Organizations*, that are considered vital. This is a highly pared down set of controls for the purposes of Industry's requirements to meet federal government cybersecurity contracting requirements. There are over 1000 potential controls offered from NIST 800-53 revision 4; this more expansive set of controls is used extensively by DOD to protect its IT systems from its jet-fighters to its vast personnel databases.

This SSP is based upon the NIST and National Archives and Records Administration (NARA) templates and provides a greater clarification to the company or agency representative, business owner, and their IT staff. This book is intended to focus business owners and their IT support staff on what is required to create and complete a **System Security Plan** (SSP) that sufficiently meets the NIST 800-171, revision 1, requirements. Companies need to focus on a "good faith" effort on how to best address these controls to the government—and, it more importantly will help the business protect its own sensitive data and Intellectual Property (IP).

In addition, the **People, Process and Technology (PPT) Model** is the recommended guidance from "Beyond DOD" for answering and responding to the controls within NIST 800-171. While all solutions will not require a **technological** answer, consideration of the **people** (e.g., who? what skill sets? etc.) and **process** (e.g., notifications to senior management, action workflows, etc.) will meet many of the response requirements. The best responses will typically include the types and kinds of people assigned to oversee the control, the process or procedures that identify the workflow that will ensure that the control is met, and in many cases, the technology that will answer the control in part or in full. (See Module #5 at Udemy.com for a free video describing the PPT Model at https://www.udemy.com/system-security-plan-ssp-for-nist-800-171-compliance/. Also, see the Access Control (AC) section that provides three examples for you and your IT staff).

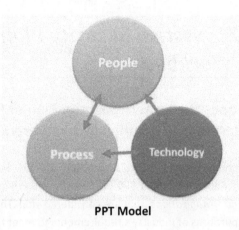

PPT Model

What's the minimum proof of a company's cybersecurity posture?

The basis of NIST 800-171 is that contractors provide adequate security on all covered contractor Information Systems (IS). Typically, the minimum requirement to demonstrate control implementation is through **documentation**. Another term that is used is an **artifact**. An artifact is any representation to an independent third-party assessor that clearly shows compliance with a specific security control. It is a major part of the proof that a business owner would provide to DOD or other federal government contract office.

The common term for the collection of all applicable and supporting artifacts is the Body of Evidence (BOE). The major items required for the BOE includes three major items:

1. **System Security Plan (SSP).** This is a standard cybersecurity document. It describes the company's overall IT infrastructure to include hardware and software lists. Where appropriate, suggestions of additional artifacts that should be included in this document and duplicated into a the standard SSP format will be recommended. The current generalized direction for the SSP is the current minimum requirement for an artifact and must also include all Plans of Actions and Milestones (POAM); the POAM is not addressed in full for the purposes of this supplement and is considered a separate artifact.

2. **Plans of Action and Milestones (POAM).** This describes any control that the company cannot fix or fully demonstrate its full compliance. It provides an opportunity for a company to delay addressing a difficult to implement technical solution or in many cases may be cost-prohibitive. (See upcoming supplement *NIST 800-171: Writing an Effective POAM* on Amazon).

Furthermore, POAMs should always have an expected completion date and defined interim milestones (typically monthly) that describe the actions leading to a full resolution or implementation of the control. **POAMs should not be for more than a year, however, a critical hint, a company may request an <u>extension</u> multiple times if unable to fully meet the control.**

3. **Company Policy** or **Procedure**. Any corporate direction provided to internal employees, subcontractors, and some third-party service providers such as Managed or Cloud Service Providers. This direction is typically enforceable under United States labor laws and Human Resource (HR) direction. It is recommended that such a policy or procedure artifact be a *singular* collection of how the company addresses each of the 110 security controls.

REMINDER: All policy or procedure requirements are best captured in a single business policy or procedure guide. This should address the controls aligned with the security control families

---

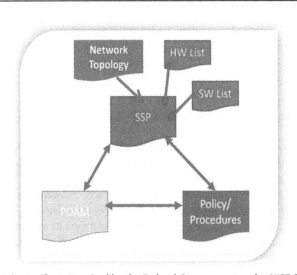

The Major Artifacts Required by the Federal Government under NIST 800-171

A little more about POAMs

The POAM is used where the business cannot meet or address the control either for technical reasons, "we don't have a Data at Rest (DAR) encryption program," or cost, "we plan to purchase the DAR solution No Later Than April 1, 2019." POAMs should include **milestones**; milestones should describe what will be accomplished over time to prepare for the full implementation of the control in the future. What will the business do in the interim to address the control? This could include, for example, other **mitigation** responses of using improved physical security controls, such as a 24-7 guard force, the addition of a steel-door to prevent entry to the main computer servers, or improved policies that have explicit repercussions upon company personnel.

POAMs will always have a defined end date. Typically, it is either within 90 days, 6 months, or a year in length. For DOD, one year should be the maximum date; however, the business, as part of this fledgling process can request an extension to the POAM past the "planned" end date. RMF affords such flexibilities; don't be afraid to exercise them as appropriate.

A CRITICAL NOTE ABOUT POAM SECURITY

How important is it to protect your POAM? It is critical that your vulnerabilities are controlled and only released to personnel who require access to the information. If the POAM listing were to become public, would-be hackers would have an easy "blueprint" of how to exploit the IT infrastructure. POAM information should always be treated as highly sensitive and the sharing of it should only be with those with a clear need-to-know. Always treat POAM information as information that should be secured in at least lockable and restricted areas both in its hard copy as well as softcopy online form.

[bracketed italicized paragraphs provide additional information on how to best approach the question or situation within an official SSP]

A free version of this NIST 800-171 SSP in a Word ® fillable template and Hardware and Software templates are also available in Excel® fillable format. They may be requested from Syber Risk LLC by emailing syber.risk.llc@gmail.com and place in the subject line: "Request for NIST 800-171 SSP, HW and SW Lists."

CONTROLLED UNCLASSIFIED INFORMATION (CUI)/
CRITICAL DEFENSE INFORMATION (CDI)[1]
[when filled in for ALL pages]

COMPANY LOGO HERE

System Security Plan (SSP) [Template]
[SYSTEM NAME "Company A Information System"> <VERSION "(1.0)"]

Report Prepared By	<Name/position>
Date of Original SSP	<Initial Submission>
Date of Latest SSP Update	<Date>

---

[1] Security markings are based on DOD standards or at the direction of the Contract Office. Non-DOD agencies should only be marked CUI. As always, confirm all security markings from your respective Contract Office.

CHANGE RECORD

Date	Description	Editor:

Background

This **System Security Plan** (SSP) is provided to meet requirements under the National Institute of Standards and Technology (NIST) Special Publication (SP) 800-171 version 1, *Protecting Controlled Unclassified Information in Nonfederal Systems and Organizations,* and the Risk Management Framework (RMF). Compliance is in accordance with applicable Federal Acquisition Regulation (FAR) and [if not a DOD contractor delete 'DFARS' portion following] Defense Federal Acquisition Regulation Supplement (DFARS) 252.204-7012 clauses. It applies to Nonfederal System Owners (NSO) and Organizations conducting business with the US Government. It applies to Information Systems (IS) to include Local Area Networks, Wide Area Networks and Interconnected Systems used in the conduct of authorized business activities with the federal government.

Applicability

The SSP is applicable to all Information Systems (IS) that store, process and/or transmit Controlled Unclassified Information (CUI)/Covered Defense Information (CDI) [for DOD contractors only] specific to NIST SP 800-171, rev 1, and any directed updates as found in the NARA CUI Registry.

---

1. SYSTEM IDENTIFICATION

1.1. System Name/Title: *[State the name of the system. Spell out acronyms. This could be as basic as "Company 'A' Information System," or "Company 'B' "Sunflower" Inventory System Database"].*

1.1.1. System Categorization: <u>Moderate for Confidentiality</u>

__1.1.1.1.__ [Confidentiality=MODERATE, Integrity and Availability are not required at this time to be categorized either by the Government or the business, respectively.

__1.1.1.2.__ This is describing that your IT system is complying with the 'moderate' security controls; this is the current standard categorization for all IS's required to comply with NIST 800-171]

1.1.2. System Unique Identifier: *[Insert any System Unique Identifier; this will be how the DOD or Federal Agency identifies the business system for "reporting" purposes.]*

1.1.3. Responsible Organization: *[Company CEO, President, or Facility Security Officer (FSO)]*

Name:	
Address:	
Phone:	

1.1.4 Information Owner *[Government POC responsible for providing and/or receiving CUI; this typically should be the designated Contract Officer Representative (COR) or assigned Contract Specialist]:*

Name:	
Title:	
Office Address:	
Work Phone:	
e-Mail Address:	

1.1.5 System Owner *[This should be a senior company officer, the assigned Chief Information Officer (CIO), or IT Program Manager responsible for managing the company's IT infrastructure.]:*

Name:	
Title:	
Office Address:	
Work Phone:	
e-Mail Address:	

***1.1.6* System Security Officer:** *[This would be typically the Information System Security Officer/Engineer (ISSO/E or Chief Information Security Officer (CISO))]:*

Name:	
Title:	
Office Address:	
Work Phone:	
e-Mail Address:	

1.2 **General Description/Purpose of System:** *[What is the function/purpose of the system? Provide a brief description of your security environment and kinds of services it provides. This could, for example, include logistics ordering, personnel records storage, or financial services. This description will help the company or agency identify what is determined as being CUI/CDI or not.]*

_____

_____

_____

1.2.3 **Number of end users and privileged users:** *[Provide the <u>approximate</u> number of users and administrators of the system. Include those with privileged access such as system administrators, database administrators, application administrators, etc. Add rows to define different roles as needed.]*

User Roles and Number of Each Type

Overall User Numbers	Number of Administrators/ Privileged Users with Elevated Privileges

1.2.4 **General Description of Information:**

1.2.4.1 *[CUI/CDI information types processed, stored, or transmitted by the system are determined and documented. For more information, see the **CUI Registry** at https://www.archives.gov/cui/registry/category-list. This will describe the types and kinds of situations when the documents, either soft or hard copy, must be properly marked and protected.*

1.2.4.2 *Typically, DOD or the respective federal agency will provide documents that are marked based upon the CUI Registry requirements. For further clarification, it is always best to document your requests for interpretation to the assigned Contracting Officer or his designated representative.*

1.2.4.3 *Document the CUI/CDI information types processed, stored, or transmitted by the system below].*

_____

_____

_____

2. SYSTEM ENVIRONMENT

2.1 Physical Network Topology:

2.1.1 **(See Module 3 for SSP on Udemy.com at https://www.udemy.com/system-security-plan-ssp-for-nist-800-171-compliance/)**

2.1.2 *[Include a detailed physical topology narrative and graphic that clearly depicts the system boundaries, system interconnections, and key devices. (Note: this does not require depicting every workstation or desktop, but include an instance for each operating system in use, an instance for portable components (if applicable), all virtual and physical servers (e.g., file, print, web, database, application), as well as any networked workstations (e.g., Unix, Windows, Mac, Linux), firewalls, routers, switches, copiers, printers, lab equipment, handhelds).*

2.1.3 *If components of other systems that interconnect/interface with this system need to be shown on the diagram, denote the system boundaries by referencing the security plans or names and owners of the other system(s) in the diagram.*

2.1.4 *Insert a system topology graphic. Provide a narrative consistent with the diagram that clearly lists and describes each system component.]*

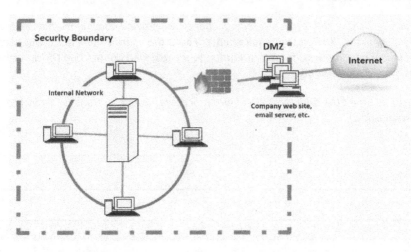

Example Physical Network Topology Diagram

2.2 Hardware Listing

2.2.1 **(See Module 2 at Udemy.com** https://www.udemy.com/system-security-plan-ssp-for-nist-800-171-compliance/ **)**

2.2.2   *[Include or reference a complete and accurate listing of all hardware (a reference to the organizational component inventory database is acceptable) and software (system software and application software) components, including make/OEM, model, version, service packs, and person or role responsible for the component.]*

2.2.3   **See Appendix A – Hardware Listing**

2.2.3.1   *[Request this template for FREE at syber.risk.llc@gmail.com]*

2.3 Software Listing

2.3.1   **See Appendix B – Software Listing**

2.3.1.1   *[Request this template for FREE at syber.risk.llc@gmail.com]*

2.4 **Hardware and Software Maintenance and Ownership** – [Is all hardware and software maintained and owned by the organization? This should address any third-party maintenance support to include Managed (external) or Cloud Service Providers(CSP).

2.4.1   *[Refer to NIST 800-171 Maintenance (MA) control discussed below. See the publication:* **NIST 800-171: Beyond DOD** *on Amazon for a detailed discussion.*

2.4.2   *If no, explain how maintenance for IS hardware and software components are generally maintained.]*

_____

_____

_____

_____

3. REQUIREMENTS

3.1 The source of these requirements is derived from the 2016 National Institute of Standards and Technology (NIST) Special Publication (SP) 800-171, revision 1, *Protecting Controlled Unclassified Information in Nonfederal Information Systems and Organizations; ensure that you are working from the 2016 Revision 1 version.*

3.2 Provide a thorough description of how all the security requirements are being implemented or planned to be implemented. The description for each security requirement contains:

1) The security requirement number and description.

2) How the security requirement is being implemented or planned to be implemented based upon the **PPT Model** as suggested in the "examples" below.

3) Any **compensating mitigations**(s) in place due to implementation constraints in lieu of the stated requirement. This may include, for example, physical security controls designed to provide specific reinforcing actions for the control or other technological solution that provides partial abilities to reduce the risk based upon this technology.

4) If the requirement is **'Not Applicable'** to the system, provide rationale that technically identifies why this control has no basis for being reviewed/assessed; this could include, for example, the application of any Wi-fi controls where the technical environment either does not have or does not allow it within the current security architecture.

Access Control (AC)

3.1.1 Limit system access to authorized users, processes acting on behalf of authorized users, and devices (including other systems).

☐ Implemented   ☐ Not Implemented -   ☐ Not Applicable
                                Planned - Requires POAM

INSTRUCTIONS: Is the control fully 'Implemented'? If the control is 'planned to be implemented' a Plan of Action and Milestone (POAM) will be required. If "Not Applicable," provide a technical rationale why the control does not apply to the IT company's IT environment.

This should describe how the control is being implemented. You should also reference where in either the SSP or a Company policy or procedure guide where the control is addressed. Assume this information is subject to audit/assessment by the Contract Office.

EXAMPLE #1: PPT Model:

1. *People: "The Company Cybersecurity procedure guide addresses the differences between the general and privileged users. Privileged users, having elevated privileges and potential "super-user" access for other users will be limited to specified IT personnel with requisite responsibilities to manage the network, and have the appropriate training.*

3. *Process: Those with elevated privileges will have, at a minimum, been appointed in writing by the Chief Information Officer (CIO) and have completed Operating System training specific to the company's current IT environment.*

4. *Technology: The company uses the Cyberark® product to further audit those with privileged access, and that information is provided to the CIO weekly."*

_____

_____

_____

_____

3.1.2 Limit system access to the types of transactions and functions that authorized users are permitted to execute.

☐ Implemented   ☐ Not Implemented -   ☐ Not Applicable
                              Planned - Requires POAM

EXAMPLE #2: PPT Model:

1. *People (general user): "This control will be addressed in the business policy/procedural document. General users are only authorized "basic" access to the company's IS system; this includes electronic mail, Internet access, and the Microsoft® business products purchased for the explicit purpose of conducting their daily duties as part of their functions to support business goals and objectives.*

2. *Process: They may not add or remove applications without following submitting a "Change Request" form developed by the Office of the CIO and verified by their 1st line supervisor and approved by the Deputy CIO for Business Operations.*

3. *Technology: The use of Bitlocker® to enforce unenforced actions will be used to both "whitelist" authorized programs and functions, and "blacklist" all unauthorized sites such as gambling, pornography, etc., will be blocked.*

4. *People (privileged user): Those with privileged access which includes, for example, back-office maintenance, network care, account creation, database maintenance, etc. will be limited to only those functions a part of*

their duties; these duties will align with the privileged users' job description for the current year.

5. Process: Privileged user access reviews will be reassessed every year. Their access will be segregated by different logins and passwords for audit purposes.

6. Technology: The company uses the Cyberark® product to further audit those with privileged access, and the audit logs will be provided to the CIO weekly."

_____

_____

_____

_____

_____

3.1.3 Control the flow of CUI in accordance with approved authorizations.

☐ Implemented   ☐ Not Implemented -   ☐ Not Applicable
                               Planned - Requires POAM

EXAMPLE #3: PPT Model:

1. People: "The company Cybersecurity procedure guide addresses that all users are required to apply built-in email encryption when transmitting CUI/CDI.

2. Process: The company uses flow control to manage the movement of CUI/CDI throughout the IT architecture; flow control is based on the types of information. Additional procedural   concerns will be addressed: 1) Only authorized personnel within the company with the requisite need-to-know are provided access; 2) All Data in Transit (DIT) will be encrypted using at a minimum the Advanced Encryption Standard (AES) 256-bit key length encryption.

3. Technology: The company uses the ABC Company Advanced Encryption Standard (AES) 256-bit key length encryption application; only this product will be used for transiting CUI/CDI."

_____

_____

_____

_____

3.1.4 Separate the duties of individuals to reduce the risk of malevolent activity without collusion.

☐ Implemented   ☐ Not Implemented -   ☐ Not Applicable
                          Planned - Requires POAM

_____

_____

_____

_____

3.1.5 Employ the principle of least privilege, including for specific security functions and privileged accounts.

☐ Implemented   ☐ Not Implemented -   ☐ Not Applicable
                          Planned - Requires POAM

_____

_____

_____

3.1.6 Use non-privileged accounts or roles when accessing nonsecurity functions.

☐ Implemented   ☐ Not Implemented -   ☐ Not Applicable
                          Planned - Requires POAM

_____

_____

_____

_____

3.1.7 Prevent non-privileged users from executing privileged functions and audit the execution of such functions.

☐ Implemented   ☐ Not Implemented -   ☐ Not Applicable
                               Planned - Requires POAM

_____

_____

_____

_____

3.1.8 Limit unsuccessful logon attempts.

☐ Implemented   ☐ Not Implemented -   ☐ Not Applicable
                               Planned - Requires POAM

_____

_____

_____

_____

3.1.9 Provide privacy and security notices consistent with applicable CUI rules.

☐ Implemented   ☐ Not Implemented -   ☐ Not Applicable
                               Planned - Requires POAM

_____

_____

_____

_____

3.1.10 Use session lock with pattern-hiding displays to prevent access and viewing of data after period of inactivity.

☐ Implemented   ☐ Not Implemented -   ☐ Not Applicable
Planned - Requires POAM

_____

_____

_____

_____

3.1.11 Terminate (automatically) a user session after a defined condition.

☐ Implemented   ☐ Not Implemented -   ☐ Not Applicable
Planned - Requires POAM

_____

_____

_____

_____

3.1.12 Monitor and control remote access sessions.

☐ Implemented   ☐ Not Implemented -   ☐ Not Applicable
Planned - Requires POAM

_____

_____

_____

_____

3.1.13 Employ cryptographic mechanisms to protect the confidentiality of remote access sessions.

☐ Implemented   ☐ Not Implemented -   ☐ Not Applicable
                                        Planned - Requires POAM

_____

_____

_____

3.1.14 Route remote access via managed access control points.

☐ Implemented   ☐ Not Implemented -   ☐ Not Applicable
                                        Planned - Requires POAM

_____

_____

_____

_____

3.1.15 Authorize remote execution of privileged commands and remote access to security-relevant information.

☐ Implemented   ☐ Not Implemented -   ☐ Not Applicable
                                        Planned - Requires POAM

_____

_____

_____

_____

3.1.16 Authorize wireless access prior to allowing such connections.

☐ Implemented   ☐ Not Implemented -   ☐ Not Applicable
                          Planned - Requires POAM

_____

_____

_____

_____

3.1.17 Protect wireless access using authentication and encryption.

☐ Implemented   ☐ Not Implemented -   ☐ Not Applicable
                          Planned - Requires POAM

_____

_____

_____

_____

3.1.18 Control connection of mobile devices.

☐ Implemented   ☐ Not Implemented -   ☐ Not Applicable
                          Planned - Requires POAM

_____

_____

_____

_____

3.1.19 Encrypt CUI on mobile devices and mobile computing platforms.

☐ Implemented ☐ Not Implemented - ☐ Not Applicable
Planned - Requires POAM

_____

_____

_____

_____

3.1.20 Verify and control/limit connections to and use of external systems.

☐ Implemented ☐ Not Implemented - ☐ Not Applicable
Planned - Requires POAM

_____

_____

_____

_____

3.1.21 Limit use of organizational portable storage devices on external systems.

☐ Implemented ☐ Not Implemented - ☐ Not Applicable
Planned - Requires POAM

_____

_____

_____

_____

3.1.22 Control CUI posted or processed on publicly accessible systems.

☐ Implemented ☐ Not Implemented - ☐ Not Applicable
Planned - Requires POAM

_____

_____

_____

_____

_____

Awareness and Training (AT)

3.2.1 Ensure that managers, systems administrators, and users of organizational systems are made aware of the security risks associated with their activities and of the applicable policies, standards, and procedures related to the security of those systems.

☐ Implemented ☐ Not Implemented - ☐ Not Applicable
Planned - Requires POAM

_____

_____

_____

_____

3.2.2 Ensure that organizational personnel are adequately trained to carry out their assigned information security-related duties and responsibilities.

☐ Implemented ☐ Not Implemented - ☐ Not Applicable
Planned - Requires POAM

_____

_____

_____

_____

3.2.3 Provide security awareness training on recognizing and reporting potential indicators of insider threat.

☐ Implemented   ☐ Not Implemented -   ☐ Not Applicable
                        Planned - Requires POAM

_____

_____

_____

_____

Audit and Accountability (AU)

3.3.1 Create and retain system audit logs and records to the extent needed to enable the monitoring, analysis, investigation, and reporting of unlawful or unauthorized system activity.

☐ Implemented   ☐ Not Implemented -   ☐ Not Applicable
                        Planned - Requires POAM

_____

_____

_____

3.3.2 Ensure that the actions of individual system users can be uniquely traced to those users, so they can be held accountable for their actions.

☐ Implemented   ☐ Not Implemented -   ☐ Not Applicable
                          Planned - Requires POAM

_____

_____

_____

_____

_____

_____

3.3.3 Review and update logged events.

☐ Implemented   ☐ Not Implemented -   ☐ Not Applicable
                          Planned - Requires POAM

_____

_____

_____

_____

3.3.4 Alert in the event of an audit logging process failure.

☐ Implemented   ☐ Not Implemented -   ☐ Not Applicable
                          Planned - Requires POAM

_____

_____

_____
_____

3.3.5 **Correlate audit record review, analysis, and reporting processes for investigation and response to indications of unlawful, unauthorized, suspicious, or unusual activity.**

☐ Implemented   ☐ Not Implemented -   ☐ Not Applicable
                                Planned - Requires POAM

_____

_____

_____

_____

3.3.6 **Provide audit record reduction and report generation to support on-demand analysis and reporting.**

☐ Implemented   ☐ Not Implemented -   ☐ Not Applicable
                                Planned - Requires POAM

_____

_____

_____

_____

3.3.7 **Provide a system capability that compares and synchronizes internal system clocks with an authoritative source to generate time stamps for audit records.**

☐ Implemented   ☐ Not Implemented -   ☐ Not Applicable
                                Planned - Requires POAM

_____

_____

_____

_____

_____

3.3.8 Protect audit information and audit logging tools from unauthorized access, modification, and deletion.

☐ Implemented   ☐ Not Implemented -   ☐ Not Applicable
                               Planned - Requires POAM

_____

_____

_____

_____

3.3.9 Limit management of audit logging functionality to a subset of privileged users.

☐ Implemented   ☐ Not Implemented -   ☐ Not Applicable
                               Planned - Requires POAM

_____

_____

_____

_____

_____

Configuration Management (CM)

3.4.1 **Establish and maintain baseline configurations and inventories of organizational systems (including hardware, software, firmware, and documentation) throughout the respective system development life cycles.**

☐ Implemented ☐ Not Implemented - ☐ Not Applicable
Planned - Requires POAM

_____

_____

_____

_____

3.4.2 **Establish and enforce security configuration settings for information technology products employed in organizational systems.**

☐ Implemented ☐ Not Implemented - ☐ Not Applicable
Planned - Requires POAM

_____

_____

_____

_____

3.4.3 **Track, review, approve or disapprove, and log changes to organizational systems.**

☐ Implemented ☐ Not Implemented - ☐ Not Applicable
Planned - Requires POAM

_____

_____

_____

_____

3.4.4 Analyze the security impact of changes prior to implementation.

☐ Implemented   ☐ Not Implemented -   ☐ Not Applicable
                          Planned - Requires POAM

_____

_____

_____

3.4.5 Define, document, approve, and enforce physical and logical access restrictions associated with changes to organizational systems.

☐ Implemented   ☐ Not Implemented -   ☐ Not Applicable
                          Planned - Requires POAM

_____

_____

_____

_____

3.4.6 Employ the principle of least functionality by configuring organizational systems to provide only essential capabilities.

☐ Implemented   ☐ Not Implemented -   ☐ Not Applicable
                          Planned - Requires POAM

_____

_____

3.4.7 Restrict, disable, or prevent the use of nonessential programs, functions, ports, protocols, and services.

☐ Implemented   ☐ Not Implemented -   ☐ Not Applicable
                                   Planned - Requires POAM

_____

_____

_____

_____

3.4.8 Apply deny-by-exception (blacklisting) policy to prevent the use of unauthorized software or deny-all, permit-by-exception (whitelisting) policy to allow the execution of authorized software.

☐ Implemented   ☐ Not Implemented -   ☐ Not Applicable
                                   Planned - Requires POAM

_____

_____

_____

_____

3.4.9 Control and monitor user-installed software.

☐ Implemented   ☐ Not Implemented -   ☐ Not Applicable
                                   Planned - Requires POAM

_____

_____

_____

_____

_____

Identification and Authentication (IA)

3.5.1 Identify system users, processes acting on behalf of users, and devices.

☐ Implemented   ☐ Not Implemented -   ☐ Not Applicable
                          Planned - Requires POAM

_____

_____

_____

_____

3.5.2 Authenticate (or verify) the identities of users, processes, or devices, as a prerequisite to allowing access to organizational systems.

☐ Implemented   ☐ Not Implemented -   ☐ Not Applicable
                          Planned - Requires POAM

_____

_____

_____

_____

3.5.3 Use multifactor authentication for local and network access to privileged accounts and for network access to non-privileged accounts.

☐ Implemented   ☐ Not Implemented -   ☐ Not Applicable
                          Planned - Requires POAM

_____

_____

_____

_____

3.5.4 Employ replay-resistant authentication mechanisms for network access to privileged and non-privileged accounts.

☐ Implemented   ☐ Not Implemented -   ☐ Not Applicable
                          Planned - Requires POAM

_____

_____

_____

_____

_____

3.5.5 Prevent reuse of identifiers for a defined period.

☐ Implemented   ☐ Not Implemented -   ☐ Not Applicable
                          Planned - Requires POAM

_____

_____

3.5.6 Disable identifiers after a defined period of inactivity.

☐ Implemented   ☐ Not Implemented -   ☐ Not Applicable
Planned - Requires POAM

_____

_____

_____

_____

3.5.7 Enforce a minimum password complexity and change of characters when new passwords are created.

☐ Implemented   ☐ Not Implemented -   ☐ Not Applicable
Planned - Requires POAM

_____

_____

_____

_____

3.5.8 Prohibit password reuse for a specified number of generations.

☐ Implemented   ☐ Not Implemented -   ☐ Not Applicable
Planned - Requires POAM

_____

_____

3.5.9 Allow temporary password use for system logons with an immediate change to a permanent password.

☐ Implemented ☐ Not Implemented - Planned - Requires POAM ☐ Not Applicable

_____

_____

_____

_____

3.5.10 Store and transmit only cryptographically-protected passwords.

☐ Implemented ☐ Not Implemented - Planned - Requires POAM ☐ Not Applicable

_____

_____

_____

_____

3.5.11 Obscure feedback of authentication information.

☐ Implemented ☐ Not Implemented - Planned - Requires POAM ☐ Not Applicable

_____

_____

_____

_____

_____

Incident Response (IR)

3.6.1 Establish an operational incident-handling capability for organizational systems that includes preparation, detection, analysis, containment, recovery, and user response activities.

☐ Implemented   ☐ Not Implemented -   ☐ Not Applicable
                          Planned - Requires POAM

_____

_____

_____

_____

3.6.2 Track, document, and report incidents to designated officials and/or authorities both internal and external to the organization.

☐ Implemented   ☐ Not Implemented -   ☐ Not Applicable
                          Planned - Requires POAM

_____

_____

_____

_____

3.6.3 Test the organizational incident response capability

☐ Implemented   ☐ Not Implemented -   ☐ Not Applicable
                          Planned - Requires POAM

_____

_____

_____

_____

Maintenance (MA)

3.7.1 Perform maintenance on organizational systems.

☐ Implemented   ☐ Not Implemented -   ☐ Not Applicable
                              Planned - Requires POAM

_____

_____

_____

_____

3.7.2 Provide controls on the tools, techniques, mechanisms, and personnel used to conduct system maintenance.

☐ Implemented   ☐ Not Implemented -   ☐ Not Applicable
                              Planned - Requires POAM

_____

_____

_____

_____

3.7.3 Ensure equipment removed for off-site maintenance is sanitized of any CUI.

☐ Implemented   ☐ Not Implemented -   ☐ Not Applicable
                                 Planned - Requires POAM

_____

_____

_____

_____

3.7.4 Check media containing diagnostic and test programs for malicious code before the media are used in organizational systems.

☐ Implemented   ☐ Not Implemented -   ☐ Not Applicable
                                 Planned - Requires POAM

_____

_____

_____

_____

3.7.5 Require multifactor authentication to establish nonlocal maintenance sessions via external network connections and terminate such connections when nonlocal maintenance is complete.

☐ Implemented   ☐ Not Implemented -   ☐ Not Applicable
                                 Planned - Requires POAM

_____

_____

_____

_____

3.7.6 Supervise the maintenance activities of maintenance personnel without required access authorization.

☐ Implemented   ☐ Not Implemented -   ☐ Not Applicable
                          Planned - Requires POAM

_____

_____

_____

_____

_____

Media Protection (MP)

3.8.1 Protect (i.e., physically control and securely store) system media containing CUI, both paper and digital.

☐ Implemented   ☐ Not Implemented -   ☐ Not Applicable
                          Planned - Requires POAM

_____

_____

_____

_____

3.8.2 Limit access to CUI on system media to authorized users.

☐ Implemented   ☐ Not Implemented -   ☐ Not Applicable
                          Planned - Requires POAM

_____

_____

_____

_____

3.8.3 Sanitize or destroy system media containing CUI before disposal or release for reuse.

☐ Implemented   ☐ Not Implemented -   ☐ Not Applicable
                                       Planned - Requires POAM

_____

_____

_____

_____

3.8.4 Mark media with necessary CUI markings and distribution limitations.

☐ Implemented   ☐ Not Implemented -   ☐ Not Applicable
                                       Planned - Requires POAM

_____

_____

_____

_____

3.8.5 Control access to media containing CUI and maintain accountability for media during transport outside of controlled areas.

☐ Implemented   ☐ Not Implemented -   ☐ Not Applicable
                                       Planned - Requires POAM

_____

_____

_____

_____

3.8.6 Implement cryptographic mechanisms to protect the confidentiality of CUI stored on digital media during transport unless otherwise protected by alternative physical safeguards.

☐ Implemented　　　　　　☐ Not Implemented -　　　☐ Not Applicable
　　　　　　　　　　　　　　Planned - Requires POAM

_____

_____

_____

_____

3.8.7 Control the use of removable media on system components.

☐ Implemented　　　　　　☐ Not Implemented -　　　☐ Not Applicable
　　　　　　　　　　　　　　Planned - Requires POAM

_____

_____

_____

_____

_____

3.8.8 **Prohibit the use of portable storage devices when such devices have no identifiable owner.**

☐ Implemented ☐ Not Implemented - ☐ Not Applicable
Planned - Requires POAM

_____

_____

_____

_____

3.8.9 **Protect the confidentiality of backup CUI at storage locations.**

☐ Implemented ☐ Not Implemented - ☐ Not Applicable
Planned - Requires POAM

_____

_____

_____

_____

Personnel Security (PS)

3.9.1 **Screen individuals prior to authorizing access to organizational systems containing CUI.**

☐ Implemented ☐ Not Implemented - ☐ Not Applicable
Planned - Requires POAM

_____

_____

3.9.2 Ensure that organizational systems containing CUI are protected during and after personnel actions such as terminations and transfers.

☐ Implemented   ☐ Not Implemented -   ☐ Not Applicable
                                    Planned - Requires POAM

Physical Protection (PP)

3.10.1 Limit physical access to organizational systems, equipment, and the respective operating environments to authorized individuals.

☐ Implemented   ☐ Not Implemented -   ☐ Not Applicable
                                    Planned - Requires POAM

3.10.2 Protect and monitor the physical facility and support infrastructure for organizational systems.

☐ Implemented ☐ Not Implemented - Planned - Requires POAM ☐ Not Applicable

_____

_____

_____

_____

3.10.3 Escort visitors and monitor visitor activity.

☐ Implemented ☐ Not Implemented - Planned - Requires POAM ☐ Not Applicable

_____

_____

_____

_____

3.10.4 Maintain audit logs of physical access.

☐ Implemented ☐ Not Implemented - Planned - Requires POAM ☐ Not Applicable

_____

_____

_____

_____

3.10.5 Control and manage physical access devices.

☐ Implemented ☐ Not Implemented - ☐ Not Applicable
Planned - Requires POAM

_____

_____

_____

_____

3.10.6 Enforce safeguarding measures for CUI at alternate work sites.

☐ Implemented ☐ Not Implemented - ☐ Not Applicable
Planned - Requires POAM

_____

_____

_____

_____

Risk Assessment (RA)

3.11.1 Periodically assess the risk to organizational operations (including mission, functions, image, or reputation), organizational assets, and individuals, resulting from the operation of organizational systems and the associated processing, storage, or transmission of CUI.

□ Implemented ☐ Not Implemented - ☐ Not Applicable
Planned - Requires POAM

_____

_____

_____

_____

3.11.2 Scan for vulnerabilities in organizational systems and applications periodically and when new vulnerabilities affecting those systems and applications are identified.

□ Implemented ☐ Not Implemented - ☐ Not Applicable
Planned - Requires POAM

_____

_____

_____

_____

3.11.3 Remediate vulnerabilities in accordance with risk assessments.

□ Implemented ☐ Not Implemented - ☐ Not Applicable
Planned - Requires POAM

_____

_____

_____

_____

Security Assessment (SA)

3.12.1 Periodically assess the security controls in organizational systems to determine if the controls are effective in their application.

☐ Implemented   ☐ Not Implemented -   ☐ Not Applicable
Planned - Requires POAM

_____

_____

_____

_____

3.12.2 Develop and implement plans of action designed to correct deficiencies and reduce or eliminate vulnerabilities in organizational systems.

☐ Implemented   ☐ Not Implemented -   ☐ Not Applicable
Planned - Requires POAM

_____

_____

_____

_____

3.12.3 Monitor security controls on an ongoing basis to ensure the continued effectiveness of the controls.

☐ Implemented   ☐ Not Implemented -   ☐ Not Applicable
Planned - Requires POAM

_____

_____

_____

_____

3.12.4 Develop, document, and periodically update system security plans that describe system boundaries, system environments of operation, how security requirements are implemented, and the relationships with or connections to other systems.

☐ Implemented   ☐ Not Implemented -   ☐ Not Applicable
                              Planned - Requires POAM

_____

_____

_____

_____

_____

System and Communications Protection (SC)

3.13.1 Monitor, control, and protect communications (i.e., information transmitted or received by organizational systems) at the external boundaries and key internal boundaries of organizational systems.

☐ Implemented   ☐ Not Implemented -   ☐ Not Applicable
                              Planned - Requires POAM

_____

_____

_____

_____

3.13.2 Employ architectural designs, software development techniques, and systems engineering principles that promote effective information security within organizational systems.

☐ Implemented   ☐ Not Implemented -   ☐ Not Applicable
                                     Planned - Requires POAM

_____

_____

_____

_____

3.13.3 Separate user functionality from system management functionality.

☐ Implemented   ☐ Not Implemented -   ☐ Not Applicable
                                     Planned - Requires POAM

_____

_____

_____

_____

3.13.4 Prevent unauthorized and unintended information transfer via shared system resources.

☐ Implemented   ☐ Not Implemented -   ☐ Not Applicable
                                     Planned - Requires POAM

_____

_____

_____

_____

3.13.5 Implement subnetworks for publicly accessible system components that are physically or logically separated from internal networks.

☐ Implemented   ☐ Not Implemented -   ☐ Not Applicable
Planned - Requires POAM

_____

_____

_____

_____

3.13.6 Deny network communications traffic by default and allow network communications traffic by exception (i.e., deny all, permit by exception).

☐ Implemented   ☐ Not Implemented -   ☐ Not Applicable
Planned - Requires POAM

_____

_____

_____

_____

3.13.7 Prevent remote devices from simultaneously establishing non-remote connections with organizational systems and communicating via some other connection to resources in external networks (i.e., split tunneling).

☐ Implemented   ☐ Not Implemented -   ☐ Not Applicable
Planned - Requires POAM

_____

_____

_____

_____

3.13.8 Implement cryptographic mechanisms to prevent unauthorized disclosure of CUI during transmission unless otherwise protected by alternative physical safeguards.

☐ Implemented   ☐ Not Implemented -   ☐ Not Applicable
                                            Planned - Requires POAM

_____

_____

_____

_____

3.13.9 Terminate network connections associated with communications sessions at the end of the sessions or after a defined period of inactivity.

☐ Implemented   ☐ Not Implemented -   ☐ Not Applicable
                                            Planned - Requires POAM

_____

_____

_____

_____

3.13.10 Establish and manage cryptographic keys for cryptography employed in organizational systems.

☐ Implemented   ☐ Not Implemented -   ☐ Not Applicable
                                            Planned - Requires POAM

_____

_____

3.13.11 Employ FIPS-validated cryptography when used to protect the confidentiality of CUI.

☐ Implemented ☐ Not Implemented - ☐ Not Applicable
Planned - Requires POAM

3.13.12 Prohibit remote activation of collaborative computing devices and provide indication of devices in use to users present at the device.

☐ Implemented ☐ Not Implemented - ☐ Not Applicable
Planned - Requires POAM

3.13.13 Control and monitor the use of mobile code.

☐ Implemented ☐ Not Implemented - ☐ Not Applicable
Planned - Requires POAM

3.13.14 Control and monitor the use of Voice over Internet Protocol (VoIP) technologies.

☐ Implemented   ☐ Not Implemented -   ☐ Not Applicable
                                    Planned - Requires POAM

3.13.15 Protect the authenticity of communications sessions.

☐ Implemented   ☐ Not Implemented -   ☐ Not Applicable
                                    Planned - Requires POAM

3.13.16 Protect the confidentiality of CUI at rest.

☐ Implemented   ☐ Not Implemented -   ☐ Not Applicable
                                    Planned - Requires POAM

_____

_____

_____

System and Information Integrity (SI)

3.14.1 Identify, report, and correct system flaws in a timely manner.

☐ Implemented   ☐ Not Implemented -   ☐ Not Applicable
                          Planned - Requires POAM

_____

_____

_____

_____

3.14.2 Provide protection from malicious code at designated locations within organizational systems.

☐ Implemented   ☐ Not Implemented -   ☐ Not Applicable
                          Planned - Requires POAM

_____

_____

_____

_____

3.14.3 Monitor system security alerts and advisories and take action in response.

☐ Implemented   ☐ Not Implemented -   ☐ Not Applicable
                          Planned - Requires POAM

_____

_____

_____

_____

3.14.4 Update malicious code protection mechanisms when new releases are available.

☐ Implemented ☐ Not Implemented - ☐ Not Applicable
Planned - Requires POAM

_____

_____

_____

_____

3.14.5 Perform periodic scans of organizational systems and real-time scans of files from external sources as files are downloaded, opened, or executed.

☐ Implemented ☐ Not Implemented - ☐ Not Applicable
Planned - Requires POAM

_____

_____

_____

_____

3.14.6 Monitor organizational systems, including inbound and outbound communications traffic, to detect attacks and indicators of potential attacks.

☐ Implemented ☐ Not Implemented - ☐ Not Applicable
Planned - Requires POAM

_____

_____

_____

_____

3.14.7 Identify unauthorized use of organizational systems.

☐ Implemented   ☐ Not Implemented -   ☐ Not Applicable
                                        Planned - Requires POAM

_____

_____

_____

_____

ANNEX A – Hardware List Example

CONTROLLED UNCLASSIFIED INFORMATION (CUI)/
CRITICAL DEFENSE INFORMATION (CDI)
[when filled in for ALL pages]

<IS System Name Here> Approved Hardware

System	Subsys Item	Manufacturer	Item	SerialNo.	Model	Type/Function	Source (Vendor, Reseller, etc.)	IA Enabled (Yes/No)
					Computers			
		HP	Laptop		8460	Laptop	HP	No
		HP	Laptop		8470	Laptop	HP	No
		HP	Laptop		8570	Laptop	HP	No
		HP	Desktop		DC8200	Desktop	HP	No
		EpicData	Terminal/Time Clock		Univieu-02	Terminal/Time Clock	EpicData	No
		TekPanel	Shared Device		550T	VNS	TekPanel	No
		TekPanel	Shared Device		460T	VNS	TekPanel	No
		TekPanel	Shared Device		420T	VNS	TekPanel	No
		Dell	Tablet		Venue 11 Pro	Tablet	Dell	No
		Panasonic	Tablet		ToughPad FZ-G1 (7130/7130J (210-	Tablet	Panasonic	
					NAS/SAN			
		EMC	NAS		VNX5700	NAS	HP	No
		HP	Tape Library		ESL G3	Tape Library	HP	No
		Brocade	Fibre Switch		DS300B	NAS Fibre Switch	EMC	No
		Overland	Tape Library		NEO 8000E	Tape library	HP	No
					Printers/Scanners			
		HP	Plotter		T1100PS	Network Plotter	HP	No
		HP	Plotter		T1120PS	Network Plotter	HP	No
		HP	Plotter		DJ1200	Network Plotter	HP	No
		HP	Plotter		T1300PS	Network Plotter	HP	No
		HP	Printer		CP5525DN	Network Printer	HP	No
		HP	Printer		CP5550	Network Printer	HP	No
		HP	Printer		CP4025	Network Printer	HP	No
		HP	Printer		LaserJet Pro 400	Personal Printer	HP	No
		Primera	CD Printer		Bravo II	CD Printer	Primera	No
		Pryor	Engraver		Marktronic 3000	Engraver	Pryor	No
		Epson	Printer		Bench Dot Stylus R2000	Personal Printer	Epson	No
		Fujitsu	Scanner		Scansnap ix500	Scanner	FUJITSU	No
		Fujitsu	Scanner		Scansnap S1500	Scanner	FUJITSU	No
					Servers			
		HP	Server		DL585-G7	Server	HP	No
		HP	Server		DL585-G8	Server	HP	No
		SUN	Server		M3000	Server	SUN	No
		McAfee	Server		MVM3100	Vulnerability Scanner	McAfee	No
		Foundstone	Server		FS1000	Server	Foundstone	No
					Network			
		Cisco	Switch		4506	Switch	Cisco	Yes
		Cisco	Switch		3750	Switch	Cisco	Yes
		Juniper	Firewall		SSG-140-SH	LKE VPN Router	Juniper	Yes
		Infoblox	DNS/DHCP		820	DNS/DHCP Appliance	Infoblox	Yes

ANNEX B – Software List Example

<IS System Name Here> Approved Software [Please remove software here not used]

'C' for Commercial Off-The-Shelf
'S' for Open Source
'G' for Government Off-The-Shelf
'F' for freeware.

Vendor	SW Purpose	Retailer	SW Type	is IA or IA Enabled	Country of Origin	NIAP Evaluated
McAfee		McAfee	C	Yes		
PTC	Graphics tool - Publications	PTC	C	No		
Microsoft Corporation	Part of Visual Studio Professional Pro Ver.; Microsoft Corporation		C	No		
AT&T	Internet connecter	AT&T	G	No		
AMD Catalyst	Graphics control	AMD w/hardware	C	No		
Autodesk, Inc	3d digital designer	Autodesk, Inc	C	No		
Autodesk, Inc	Part of AutoCAD 2011 - English	Autodesk, Inc	C	No		
Autolt Team	automation language	Autolt Team	F	No		
Avecto		Avecto	C	No		
DoD	Classification Banner Display	DoD	G	Yes		
Microsoft Corporation		Microsoft Corporation	C	No		
Jetico Inc.	Data Erasure	Jetico Inc.	C	No		
Scooter Software	File/Folder Mgmt	Scooter Software	C	No		
Biscom	Fax	Biscom		No		

ABOUT THE AUTHOR

Mr. Russo is currently the Senior Information Security Engineer within the Department of Defense's (DOD) F-35 Joint Strike Fighter program. He has an extensive background in cybersecurity and is an expert in the Risk Management Framework (RMF) and DOD Instruction 8510.01 which implements RMF throughout the DOD and federal government. He holds both a Certified Information Systems Security Professional (CISSP) certification and a CISSP in information security architecture (ISSAP). He holds a 2017 certification as a Chief Information Security Officer (CISO) from the National Defense University, Washington, DC. He retired from the US Army Reserves in 2012 as the Senior Intelligence Officer.

He is the former CISO at the Department of Education where in 2016 he led the effort to close over 95% of the outstanding US Congressional and Inspector General cybersecurity shortfall weaknesses spanning as far back as five years.

Mr. Russo is the former Senior Cybersecurity Engineer supporting the Joint Medical Logistics Development Functional Center of the Defense Health Agency (DHA) at Fort Detrick, MD. He led a team of engineering and cybersecurity professionals protecting five major Medical Logistics systems supporting over 200 DOD Medical Treatment Facilities around the globe.

Mr. Russo was the Chief Technology Officer at the Small Business Administration (SBA). He led a team of over 100 IT professionals in supporting an intercontinental Enterprise IT infrastructure and security operations spanning 12-time zones; he deployed cutting-edge technologies to enhance SBA's business and information sharing operations supporting the small business community. Mr. Russo was the first-ever Program Executive Officer (PEO)/Senior Program Manager in the Office of Intelligence & Analysis at Headquarters, Department of Homeland Security (DHS), Washington, DC. Mr. Russo was responsible for the development and deployment of secure Information and Intelligence support systems for OI&A to include software applications and systems to enhance the DHS mission. He was responsible for the program management development lifecycle during his tenure at DHS.

He holds a Master of Science from the National Defense University in Government Information Leadership with a concentration in Cybersecurity and a Bachelor of Arts in Political Science with a minor in Russian Studies from Lehigh University. He holds Level III Defense Acquisition certification in Program Management, Information Technology, and Systems Engineering. He has been a member of the DOD Acquisition Corps since 2001.

*He is the author of 2018 cybersecurity publication **Understanding Your Responsibilities to Meet NIST 800-171**, a decisive and in-depth how-to book on understanding what NIST 800-171 security controls truly mean and how to best address them based upon over 25 years as a security and intelligence professional. It's about making the cryptic, comfortable ™. These are plain-English solutions to the challenges of new Federal Government cybersecurity contract requirements.*

www.ingramcontent.com/pod-product-compliance
Lightning Source LLC
LaVergne TN
LVHW092352060326
832902LV00008B/984

* 9 7 8 1 9 8 0 5 2 9 9 9 6 *